Quick Practical Studies

for Christian Teachers

Loma Meyer

CPH®

Concordia Publishing House

Edited by Arnold E. Schmidt

Contents

Introduction

Quick Practical Studies for Teachers provides a variety of helps for teachers of the faith in Sunday school, vacation Bible school, midweek school, and other educational settings. The variety of subjects enables individuals and groups to focus on issues of particular interest. These topics can be used for group or individual study.

Group Study

Most topics are covered in two pages. The first page provides background material for the leader, and the second page contains process material for the participants. Permission is granted to photocopy the Participant Page for group discussion. We recommend the following:

In Advance

1. Examine the material and plan the group process.
2. Photocopy the Participant Page for each person.
3. Gather other materials you will need.

During the Session (15–30 minutes)

1. Begin with prayer and the introductory activity.
2. Lead a discussion and group activities based on the leader notes and the Participant Page.
3. Close with prayer.

Individual Study

Teachers who cannot participate in group discussions will benefit from personal study of the topics in this book. Many of the questions and suggested activities may have great value even if done alone. The following practices can help individuals expand the benefits:

- Discuss the topic with another teacher who is working alone. Meet briefly (for example, after class on a Sunday or during the week at a restaurant), or simply use the phone or e-mail to hold discussions.
- Photocopy the Participant Pages and work together with another teacher to complete the activities.
- Discuss the topics with your pastor, director of Christian education, or Sunday school superintendent, or with another educator.

May God bless your study—and especially the teaching that follows.

The Editor

1 *Prayer*

GOAL: To grow in understanding of prayer and in skills to lead meaningful prayers in a group setting.

Introduction & Background

Pretend that you as a group are to write a congregational prayer that will be placed into the cornerstone of your new church (or into a time capsule) to be opened 250 years in the future. What would you put into your prayer so people 250 years from now could get a glimpse of life and needs today? How might a prayer 250 years from now be different from a prayer today? How might it be the same?

Prayer has been an important part of life throughout the ages. It will continue to be so in the future. Even though we pray daily in private settings, we may panic when asked "on the spot" to lead an opening, closing, or another prayer.

Prayer is an integral part of the spiritual life of a Christian. It has been called the heartbeat of our faith, our part of a conversation with God. (God's part of the conversation comes in His Word.) Prayers can be spoken, sung, or unspoken thoughts and meditations. We've prayed the Lord's Prayer many times and we know it to be a model prayer given to us by our Lord (Matthew 6:9–13; Luke 11:2–4).

Many things motivate us to pray. God invites us to do so (Psalm 50:15). He promises to hear us (John 9:31; Proverbs 15:8). We pray for our own and our neighbor's needs (Isaiah 26:16; Luke 18:13). We may bring any request to God (Mark 11:24; Philippians 4:6; 1 John 5:14).

Use the topical studies in this book to give willing participants an opportunity to lead prayers in a group setting. Ask someone to begin each session with prayer.

Their first thoughts may race to the wonderful, reflective times they have had in personal prayer. They can begin by transferring this experience to public prayer. However, most Christians look for ways to organize their prayers. A 40-year-old man said recently, "I need help. I want to pray to God, but what do I say?"

God does not ask us to follow a prescribed formula when we pray. A prayer can be a song, rhyme, or thought, one word, one sentence, one page, or longer. Christians use a variety of patterns to structure their prayers.

ACTS. Use this simple acronym to remind yourself to speak words of *adoration, confession, thanksgiving,* and *supplication* to God.

A 12-step outline provides a structure for an extended period of private prayer. Select four to six of the following steps for public prayer: *praise; waiting* (telling God, "I love You"); *confession; recalling Scripture promises; watching* (praying for protection [for country, children, etc.] from the evil one); *intercession for others; petitions for self; thanksgiving; singing; meditation* (focusing on one of God's promises); *listening; praise.*

Suggest to participants that they model prayers for their classes and help students follow those models. As children grow older, they may be able to follow a new model from time to time. In Philippians 4:6, St. Paul encourages us, "Do not be anxious about anything, but in everything, by prayer and petition, with thanksgiving, present your requests to God."

Prayer

God Speaks

1. What characterizes the relationship we can have with the Father because of Jesus? See John 16:23–27. We pray to the triune God in the name of Jesus, our advocate. What does it mean to pray in Jesus' name?
2. See Psalm 103:1; 107:1; 56:1; Philippians 4:6; and 2 Corinthians 9:15. What other thoughts will you want to include in your prayer?
3. Why do we consider the Lord's Prayer to be a model prayer?

We Respond

1. When did you first learn to pray? Did someone help you? Write your definition of prayer.
2. As a group, write a prayer that could be used to lead the opening of these topic discussions. Utilize the acronym *ACTS* or use another form.
3. Identify some ways you can help children develop a deeper understanding of prayer. For example, you might have them write responses to sentence stems such as these:
   a. Thank You, Lord, for being with me through …
   b. I praise You, Lord, for giving me …
   c. Thank You, Lord, for …
   d. Bless my Sunday school teacher (name) for …
4. Plan activities you will use with your class. Use the following as discussion starters:
   - Discuss and apply selected Scripture passages.
   - Use prayer requests from students.
   - After beginning a prayer, invite students to add their prayer requests.
   - Select one student from the class as the special "prayer child" of the week. Give each member of the class an object such as a paper heart, and have them write the name of the "prayer child" on the heart to wear for that week. In addition to being a prayer reminder, this object could serve as a witness to others with whom the children come in contact during the week.

2 Varying Your Presentation Style

GOAL: To explore ways in which learning can be enhanced through varying the presentation style.

Introduction & Background

Form groups of two or three participants. Ask groups to recall and tell about the best lecture they have ever heard; the best telling of a Bible story; the best use of puppets; the best use of discussion in teaching; the best experience that actively involved learners; and the best role playing.

Most groups will be able to recall an experience that deserves to be "best" in each category above. Teachers can be effective with a wide variety of educational techniques. This variety enhances interest among the learners. It also requires creativity on the part of the teacher.

Thus, for this topic we link together *varying your teaching style* and *creativity.* Creativity derives from the word *creative.* A creative individual creates rather than imitates. The level of creativity depends upon the amount of imitation. (Less imitation = more creativity.) Most generally, we build on something already there by adding some new twists and turns.

Varying the teaching style and being creative with children will depend on
* the students' previous experiences, interests, skill levels, and level of maturity;
* the teacher's skills and the resources available;
* the season of the year and the weather; and
* the physical properties of your classroom. For example, for arts and crafts projects, do you have a washable floor, are you near a sink, and do you have storage space? Does the room have adequate floor space for active learning involvement?

If you have 60 minutes for a Sunday school lesson, divide your session into short time slots, perhaps 5 to 15 minutes each (depending on the age of the students and other factors), and make sure you alternate kinds of activities between time slots. Of course, plan more than two kinds of activities for each hour!

Many teachers find the following practices to be helpful:
* Recruit someone to assist with art projects, crafts, and drama.
* Gather all of the materials together before the session begins and have them well organized in sequence of use.
* Correlate the type of activity with the topic.
* Evaluate your variations to be sure they enhance the teaching/learning goals. Don't be so creative that students miss the main focus of the lesson.
* Give careful thought to management techniques.
* Be sure students are clear on what you expect from them.

Do not fall into the trap of thinking variety and creativity need to run rampant and that structure is inhibitive. Strive for a balance. The variety of presentations and activities will flourish best when the planning permits individual thinking and when you provide a framework in which to work.

Develop activities and presentations to reinforce the concepts, goals, and objectives of the lesson. The teacher has the right to be flexible in changing ideas and to alter the original plan if a barrier surfaces. Use variety to make the learning more meaningful, more memorable, more individualized, and more alive. Variety serves as a way to bring out the special talents of children, to relate the concepts to the special gifts that God has given us, to help give better understanding of His will, and to increase our spiritual understandings.

Varying Your Presentation Style

God Speaks

In Ephesians 3:8–9 Paul says he was given the grace to "make plain to everyone" the unsearchable riches of Christ. How can variety in your teaching style help you do this for your class?

We Respond

1. We sometimes tire of listening after 20 minutes or so and drift off into dreamland. Many children have a much shorter attention span. We can help maintain their attention and interest through active involvement and variety in teaching and learning. List four different ways to present the Bible story in your class next Sunday morning (just the story; do not include application time):

   a.

   b.

   c.

   d.

2. Think of your hour of class time (or whatever time you have). That hour should include a variety of teaching and learning segments (such as teacher time, student time, application time, activity time, and reinforcement time). Outline an hour of your class time to demonstrate the variety used or that could be used.

3. Evaluate and discuss the following statements:
   a. Only that specific child can create a picture or idea in his or her mind. (When viewing a finished art product, it is better to ask, "Would you tell me about it?" than "What is it?")

   b. Children build on their experiences; they may release their emotions so that feelings as well as ideas are present in their art, drama, or music.
   c. Words put to music help children learn and remember better than only hearing the words.

4. Children who cannot read or write may be able to interpret their Bible story through a scribble story. The teacher tells the story, and the children scribble lines, stopping when the teacher pauses and starting a new scribble when the teacher continues. Reinforce the story by having children use their scribble stories to retell the Bible story. What preparations would you make for using scribble stories?

5. Act out a Bible story selected by the group. How helpful was the activity in reinforcing the story for adults? At what ages would this practice be most effective?

6. Plan a session in which each teacher is prepared to share or demonstrate two creative ideas for teaching arts and crafts, drama, or music. Have the group discuss how that particular idea can help to make a Bible story more meaningful in their particular class.

   For ideas for variety in presentation, see resources such as *Sure Can Use a Little Good News: 12 Gospel Plays in Rhyme,* by Jeffrey A. Burkart (CPH, 1996); *The SONday School Book: Ideas and Techniques for Teaching the Faith,* by Jeffrey A. Burkart (CPH, 1993); and *Bible Story Skitlets,* by Sandra Collier and Jean Bruns (CPH, 1998).

Participant Page **2**

3 *Storytelling*

GOAL: To become aware of the characteristics and skill of storytelling.

Introduction & Background

Ask each participant to share a personal event of the last week or two with a partner. When sharing is complete, talk about how they have just finished telling a story or part of a story. Why was this easy to do?

Storytelling has a long history. We read of storytellers of long ago, some with musical instruments on their backs, crossing cultural lines and spreading stories all over the world. After the invention of the printing press, many looked to the written word to pass along their stories.

However, the art of storytelling did not die. As a matter of fact, the ancient art of storytelling is experiencing a renaissance. After staring at computer and television screens for many hours, people hunger for the immediacy and intimacy provided by the storyteller. They want to connect. One five-year-old told her Sunday school teacher, "Tell me a story from your face." An intimacy develops when no book serves as a barrier between the teacher and the listener.

Jesus was a master storyteller. He demonstrated this in the parables He told. Jesus used a variety of stories—simple, complex, symbolic, filled with action, meaningful. Each teacher is a potential storyteller. God has given them talents so they may tell the biblical stories to their students with a special meaning for their lives.

Storytelling does not require props, though we may choose to use them. Some of the best storytellers use only their voice, vocabulary, and gestures to make the story come alive. Most storytellers, however, add variety to their presentations.

Some storytellers ask questions throughout the story to keep the group involved. (See chapter 4, "Asking Questions," for further elaboration.)

After telling the story, ask students to act it out. Or tell a story through a series of "freeze frames." Have students take an action pose and "freeze" (hold) it while the teacher tells the pertinent part of the story. Stop the "freeze" when the scene changes.

Teachers may want to become storytelling partners. They can tell the story to one another and then discuss the meaning for their lives.

Storytelling

God Speaks

Read Matthew 8:23–27, a short story about Jesus calming a storm. Where is the climax? How did the disciples feel? How did Jesus feel? How does this story apply to you?

We Respond

1. Storytelling does not require memorization, but it does require preparation. One needs to be very familiar with the story before presenting it to an audience. Pray that the Holy Spirit will guide you as you tell the story. Consider using the following steps:

    a. Read the biblical account several times. If possible, also read the account in a Bible storybook. Compare that story with the biblical record.

    b. Close the book(s). List mentally the sequence of events; make an outline in your mind. Reread the biblical account, noting any important points that you failed to outline in your mind. You may want to make an outline on a 3 × 5 card as a prop for your first few presentations. Do not fabricate something that did not happen, but do include enough descriptions to make the story come "alive." Use strong and descriptive words, words that paint pictures in the minds of children. Words are for the storyteller what notes are for the musician or colors for the artist.

    c. Go over the main sequence of events again. Look for the beginning, the body of the story (in which the characters and events of the story are developed), the climax, and the ending. Think about the meaning of the events for your life and for the lives of the class members. How can you make the story more meaningful?

    d. Watch yourself tell the story in a mirror or videotape your story for self-evaluation. Watch your facial expressions and gestures. Listen for the quality and pitch of your voice. Critique yourself or have a good friend critique your presentation with you.

    e. Change your vocal pitch, hand gestures, and posture to differentiate between characters. For example, when speaking the dialogue for a specific character, look each time at a specific corner or place in the room. Change the tempo of your story. Think of what a dreary performance it would be if the whole symphony were played at the same tempo! Some movements are slow and leisurely. During the action time, it is natural to hurry the tempo. Use pauses in effective ways to highlight certain points.

    f. Maintain eye contact with your audience. Use an appropriate voice pitch at a pleasing rate.

    g. Be relaxed and easy. Live the story. In the first telling of the story, ask the children to hold questions until the story is completed. In retelling the story, build in opportunities for the children to ask questions, finish the sentences, repeat phrases with you, or use actions.

2. Practice storytelling in a small group. Select a parable of Jesus that you feel would be effective for storytelling.

    a. Make an outline you could use while telling the story. Check your outline with a partner and make suggestions to one another.

    b. Videotape your telling of a story. Did you use pauses effectively? How did your voice indicate the climax? Did you speak too slow or too fast? Did your voice convey the emotions of the story? Report your evaluation, if you choose, at your next class session. Your analysis may be helpful for other participants.

4 Asking Questions

GOAL: To understand and be able to use the levels of questioning.

Introduction & Background

Have participants read Luke 10:25–37. Tell them to note the kinds of questions you ask about the passage. Talk about the appropriate question later, when you discuss the types of questions teachers may ask. **What did the expert in the law ask Jesus?** *(Literal question.)* **What did he indicate by his answer to Jesus in verse 27?** *(Inferential question.)* **What problem did he have after verse 37?** *(Evaluation question.)* **What do you learn from the parable of the Good Samaritan?** *(Appreciation question.)*

Curriculum resources for teaching a religion lesson usually begin with printed objectives, or a lesson focus. These are like a compass. They set our direction and help us reach our goal. Each *Our Life in Christ* Sunday school focus begins "By God's grace and by the power of the Spirit through the Word." We do not have the power to bring all of these objectives to fruition in a perfect manner. Yet we know that God promises in Isaiah 55:10 not to let His Word return to Him empty. It will accomplish His purposes.

The art of questioning can help us focus on our objectives. Questions are instruments God gives us to scatter His seed. They are an effective way to guide thinking, to clarify the text, and to make it more meaningful. Jesus asked and answered questions. In Luke 2:46–47 we read "After three days they found Him in the temple courts, sitting among the teachers, listening to them and asking them questions. Everyone who heard Him was amazed at His understanding and His answers."

Various educators have categorized questions, developed questioning taxonomies, and used other means to help us become more effective in the art of questioning. Below is an adaptation of several taxonomies:

- *Literal:* These questions focus on information that is explicitly stated in the text. These questions can have short answers like *yes, no, true,* or *false,* or they can call for more complex factual information from the text. (Answers are in the text.)
- *Inferential*: These questions ask for thinking and creativity that go beyond the printed page. For example, the student may be asked to use personal experience to make an inference or connection related to some information given in the text. (Answers are not explicit in the text, but the participant can make some connection.)
- *Evaluation*: These questions require evaluative thinking and judgment. The student compares thoughts and ideas in the text with external criteria based on his or her own information or value system. (Answers, for the most part, are in the participant's mind.)
- *Appreciation*: These questions may involve all of the three above types of thinking, but they also ask the participant to look at the relevance and value of the subject for his/her own life and experiences. (Answers are to be applied in the participant's life.)

In all of the above, the questions must be clear; the participant must receive a clear message of what is being asked. Questions help the leader accomplish the goal and objectives of the lesson.

Asking Questions

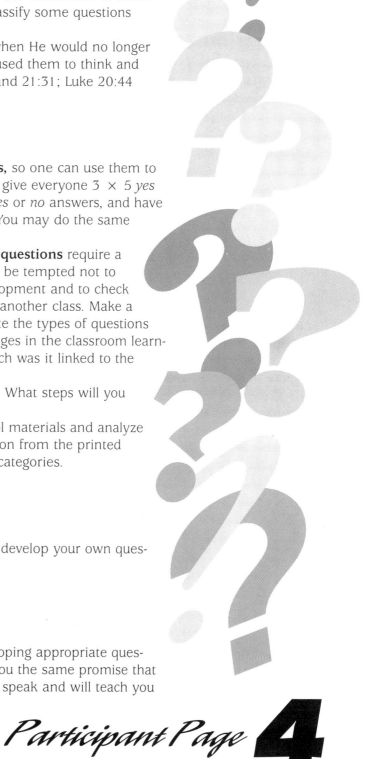

God Speaks

1. Jesus asked different kinds of questions in different situations during His ministry. In Luke 20:24 He asked a literal question: "Show me a denarius. Whose portrait and inscription are on it?" In Luke 24:26 He asked an evaluation question: "Did not the Christ have to suffer these things and then enter His glory?" Classify some questions Jesus asked at other times.
2. Jesus prepared His disciples for the time when He would no longer be with them. He asked questions that caused them to think and reason. See, for example, Matthew 16:26 and 21:31; Luke 20:44 and 22:17.

We Respond

1. Most children can answer **literal questions,** so one can use them to get the whole class involved. For example, give everyone 3 × 5 *yes* and *no* cards. Ask questions that require *yes* or *no* answers, and have students hold up the corresponding card. You may do the same thing with *true* and *false* cards.
2. **Inferential, evaluation,** and **appreciation questions** require a higher level of maturity. Therefore we may be tempted not to use them. To build your professional development and to check your ability to utilize these questions, visit another class. Make a checklist and observe, analyze, and evaluate the types of questions asked and the responses given. What changes in the classroom learning atmosphere did you observe? How much was it linked to the types of questions asked?
3. Developing questions is a challenging task. What steps will you take to make them work?
4. Look at a prepared lesson of Sunday school materials and analyze the printed questions. Write down a question from the printed materials to demonstrate each of the four categories.
   Literal:
   Inferential:
   Evaluation:
   Appreciation:
5. Select a specific Sunday school lesson and develop your own questions at each of the four levels.
   Literal:
   Inferential:
   Evaluation:
   Appreciation:

Look to God for the help you need in developing appropriate questions for each person in your class. God gives you the same promise that He gave Moses in Exodus 4:12: "I will help you speak and will teach you what to say."

Participant Page **4**

5 Using Games Effectively

GOAL: To gain understanding of the role of games in Sunday school and to gain skill in making these games relevant.

Introduction & Background

Have participants line up according to the geographical location where they were born (East Coast to West Coast). Encourage talking while the group is lining up. When everyone is in place, ask them to read 1 Corinthians 1:27 together: "God chose the foolish things of the world to shame the wise; God chose the weak things of the world to shame the strong."

Ask, **Did it seem foolish to you to line up as we just did? Why or why not? Did it help us get to know one another just a bit better? What does Paul mean when he says that the foolish and lowly things will shame the wise and strong?**

Do some students in your class act like Sunday school has become boring, dry, tiresome, monotonous, dull, no fun, the same old thing every week? Could a "foolish" and fun game make a difference?

The story of God's love for us and the wonderful gift of His Son to save us from our sins is not boring or tiresome or dull. To many of us, it continues to be the most exciting and hopeful story in the world. And yet the mere repetition of Bible stories and Bible truths, even though rich in meaning, may not be enough for the adventurous spirits of the young. Their minds are filled with the "exciting" things of this world—movies, television, baseball, football, computer games, and so on. How can Sunday school compete? Could games be part of the answer?

If used primarily for entertainment, games are *not* the answer. However, games can be part of the answer when they help accomplish class goals. We can use games to develop a better working knowledge of the Bible, to teach and reinforce biblical concepts, and to build Christian community. Fun and adventure are secondary to this aim.

A game should not be planned solely for itself, but should be used in conjunction with and as a way to help carry out the goals and objectives of the lesson. Games help to teach. They do not take the place of the lesson.

One of the first physical interactions of many children during their early months is the game of peek-a-boo. The first attempt at this game may frighten the child, but this fear soon disappears. We then see giggling and enjoyment on the part of both persons involved. Games continue to be an important part in the child's life. Children tend to play make-believe and other games until ages six or seven. Team and individualized games follow.

Following are some times in a typical Sunday school class when games may be appropriate (dependent on the game):

- While the children are assembling or waiting for something to be prepared.
- When preparing to teach a concept or as a culmination activity to reinforce the objective of the lesson.
- During the lesson time to teach or reinforce a concept.

The following resources can help teachers plan games:

Chalkboard Games for the Christian Classroom by Anita Reith Stohs (CPH, 12-3275)

File Folder Games for the Christian Classroom by Margaret Shauers (CPH, 12-3388)

Celebration Centers A–M (CPH, 12-3369) and *N–Z* (CPH, 12-3368) by Jane Haas

"Electronic Game Boards," *The SONday School Book: Ideas and Techniques for Teaching the Faith,* pp. 131–4, by Jeffrey A. Burkart (CPH, 12-3253)

Using Games Effectively

God Speaks

Children are not always as attentive as we hope they will be, in spite of all our planning. Write down three concepts from chapters 3 and 4 of 2 Corinthians that encourage you in your teaching.

We Respond

1. Create a game that reinforces the Chinese proverb "If I see, I forget. If I hear, I remember. If I do, I learn." Explain the game to the group.
2. Think of a game for your age level and identify ways to use that game. Focus on group games, but feel free to use some individual or partner-type games to respond to individual differences or for those who always finish early or come early.
3. Which of the following will provide the best evaluation tool as you determine if a game has been successful?
   a. Listen to the chatter; are students cooperating? sharing? bickering?
   b. Do students look accepted or rejected? (If rejected, where did the structure break down?)
   c. At the culmination of the lesson, were the goals of the lesson reinforced by the game?

Game Ideas

1. We can divide games into broad categories such as the following:
   a. Crossword puzzles or hidden-word puzzles.
   b. Games such as 20 Questions, Charades, Who Am I? or Pictionary.
   c. Board games (for example, a game that depicts the journey of Mary, Joseph, and Jesus to escape Herod's mandate that all babies under two should be killed).
   d. Bible baseball.
   e. Electronic game boards.
   f. Adaptations of games like Concentration.

2. *Bible Jeopardy.* Participants work in teams and have Bibles. Give each group a theme of the Bible such as *parables, miracles, books of the Bible, women in the Bible, places in the Bible,* or *prophets in the Bible.* Each team develops questions and answers similar to the Jeopardy television show.
3. *Guessing Game.* Base the game on the day's lesson. Write key words or names of actual objects from the lesson on little slips of paper to place in a hat or box. Players draw out a slip of paper, read it, and then sketch it on the board or on a chart. Group members try to guess what it is. Take turns until everyone has a chance to draw. The group can be divided into teams.
4. *Adaptation of Simon Says.* You may use this with a class of preschool or primary children. One student will begin as the leader. Select two names used in the Bible stories covered. For example, the class can be instructed to do an action when the leader says, "Joseph says," but not for "Potiphar says." The child who responds to "Potiphar says" becomes the next leader.
5. *Memory Beanbag.* Have each child print one of the memory verses for a quarter or month on a separate piece of paper. Spread these out on the floor. Children take turns tossing beanbags to land on the Bible verses. They say the verse they hit.

6 *Interactive/Integrated Learning*

GOAL: To grow in the ability to apply interactive/integrated learning.

Introduction & Background

Ask participants to tell about a time during their childhood they were taught something they no longer remember well. Next talk about things they do remember. What was the difference? Often the second kind of learning has more application to real life.

As methods of education change in day schools, student expectations for the Sunday school hour also change. Two related changes involve interactive learning and integrated learning.

Interactive learning implies reciprocal teaching/learning. The teacher gives leadership, but the students are active rather than passive listeners. They interact with the teacher through discussions, questions, and other active-type responses.

Integrated learning unites a wide variety of application fields with the Scripture lesson. Teachers link learnings inside of the classroom with learnings on the outside.

The *Our Life in Christ* Teachers Guide (Junior level, March–May 1998, p. 4) defines interactive learning experiences as involving "class members working with a partner or within a small grouping of students. Interactive activities may include, but are not limited to: roleplays, physical challenges, games, and Bible-study experiences. Students interact more openly within a partnership or small group. No one is left watching—everyone gets involved!"

No artificial divisions of knowledge separate interactive/integrated education from real life. The subject of a Sunday morning lesson is not an add-on; rather, it is a focus on finding the answers to questions for our lives. Small groups can be formed to maximize interaction.

The activities are designed to enable students to understand and apply the concept or skill emphasized by the lesson.

Integrative teaching/learning grew from dissatisfaction with schooling that involved rote memorization of facts, the lecture method, and little or no application. In real life, the separate pieces of a puzzle affect other parts. We use knowledge and skills together to help solve a problem.

Interactive/integrated learning provides opportunities to study a particular question in-depth by looking at it from a number of different angles, such as using a number of different passages from Scripture. All is coordinated—the telling or reading of the Bible story, special projects, group discussions, games, and so forth. We want to engage the whole learner. By this we mean the heart, the mind, and the spirit.

In *Changing Hearts, Changing Lives* (CPH, 1997, p. 67), Jane Fryar identifies some of the ways we learn best. A lesson becomes interactive and integrated for the learner

- when they see the value for their lives of the material to be learned;
- when the lesson begins with some kind of activity to engage the learner—to help them make a smooth transition from their everyday lives into the lesson material;
- when learning activities are hands-on, not just theoretical or "heady";
- when the learning task engages all five senses or as many of these as are practical (in contrast to simply listening);
- when the learner interacts with others, evaluates ideas, discusses observations, explores new truths, and thinks through the implications of those truths;
- when what they learn is meaningful to them, and when they can put it to use in their lives right away.

Interactive/Integrated Learning

God Speaks

How do James 3:13 and 1 Corinthians 13:11–13 connect with interactive/integrated learning? How do you recognize a wise person? What application do these passages have for you and your classes?

We Respond

1. Evaluate your lessons with these points in mind: How will my students be changed by this lesson? Will they think or act differently? Will they be drawn closer to Jesus? Did the lesson connect to life?

2. What was the theme of your last lesson? Did the central theme continue to be emphasized in the lesson? If not, why not? If need be, how can this be changed?

3. Take off one shoe. On an 8½ × 11-inch or 8½ × 14-inch sheet of paper, trace around your foot. Place the tracing in front of you. If the foot could talk, what would it remember about today? Did your foot cause you to do any interactive/integrated learning, or was it engaged only in isolated facts? Did its activities keep you, by the grace of God, on the road to everlasting life? Where was its most joyful place? Why? Where do you think the foot will take you in your future?

4. In *Get Active: Active Teaching Ideas for Lifetime Learning,* Kurt Bickel uses a four-step process to integrate a lesson. On pages 73–75 he provides this primary-grade example:

Concept: Creation. When we explore God's world, we discover how wonderful He is! "The heavens declare the glory of God; the skies proclaim the work of His hands" (Psalm 19:1).

Step 1—Activity. ("Do It"): You will need cardboard boxes the size of shoe boxes or larger—one box for every two children in your class. Also, bring a variety of materials from nature such as rocks, leaves, shells, feathers, plants, seeds, pine cones, tree bark, and flowers.

Divide the class into pairs of children. Tell them, "You are going to play a guessing game with each other. One of you will look to see what is in the box. The other will have to guess what is in the box. The person who is guessing will have to ask questions about God's creation to discover what's in the box. The person who looks in the box may only answer questions with yes or no."

Switch sides and play a second time. Add new items to the boxes.

For the third round the pair needs to look for something very unique about each item. "Be ready to tell the class about it."

Step 2—Process. (What?) Bring all the class together. Invite the pairs to tell about their items, one pair at a time. This will be like show and tell with the items they have just discovered.

Step 3—Connection. (So What?) The Bible says that the creation declares the glory of God. That means that even silent things have a message from our heavenly Father. Ask, "Can you hear a message from the items you studied?" Write student responses on a large sheet titled "Silent Message."

Step 4—Application. (Now What?) Give each child a 3 × 5 index card with a hole punched in the center. Tell them that this can be a special viewer to see God's world. It helps you see just a small portion of something. Practice using the card to look at a small part of a larger item. Tell the class, "This week I would like you to look at three things with this viewer. Let me know what you discover. What did you learn about God's creation?"

Participant Page 6

7 Making Curriculum Choices

GOAL: To help teachers make choices in curriculum.

Introduction & Background

Give each teacher a complete set of Sunday school, vacation Bible school, or other curriculum materials for their level. Ask them to examine the choices listed in the teachers guide. Which activities seem especially appropriate? Which would they want to omit or revise? What kinds of adaptations would they make?

Gone are the days when teachers had little besides pen, pencil, paper, and a copy of the Bible for teaching. Teachers now have access to complete sets of colorful and graphic materials with hands-on activities for all age levels, from newborns into adulthood. Teachers guides and packets with hands-on projects, craft packets, videos and video segments, and story/song cassettes provide valuable helps to the teacher.

Teachers begin their preparation with a study of the biblical text for the day. They continue lesson preparation with a careful evaluation and study of the teachers guide. What are the goals and objectives of the lesson? How can they be met? The method of presentation can be a teacher choice. It depends upon the needs of the group, the instructional surroundings, and the characteristics of the teacher.

Discuss the importance of teacher/student relationships and trust in a classroom situation. In some cases these may be as important as the facts of a lesson. They surely will serve as a bridge to help students gain from the lesson and grow in their relationship to God and to you.

Teachers need to consider a number of factors when choosing activities. These include *the students, the teacher, the administration,* and *the setting.* Here are some starters to help meet the challenge:

- Build on what the children know.
- Involve students in planning how to handle a lesson.
- Have students build a web of information that they already know about the story, and later fill in the missing parts.
- Invite students to watch for a part of the lesson that they will share with a younger class.
- Emphasize the applications of the lesson.
- Individualize the materials.
- Have a computer guru in your congregation develop computer games or computer materials that follow the curriculum and meet individual differences.
- Use some of the religious computer software already available.
- Divide your class into two sections for part of the hour; then bring them together for community building for the last part of the session.
- Use a variety of audiovisual materials, or bring in outside speakers.
- Hold a meeting of professional and volunteer teachers to plan ways to meet your challenges.

Making Curriculum Choices

God Speaks

As we teach, God wants us to make disciples of all nations. Read Matthew 28:19–20. What does it mean to you? How can you apply this to your life? Curriculum materials serve as tools for teachers.

We Respond

Good teaching involves making choices. This enables us to meet individual challenges as we teach. We need to consider at least four factors when making choices:

1. **The students.** Individuals vary widely. How would you respond to the following situations?
   - You have 10 students in your sixth-grade class. Seven of them study religion in a school setting and three do not. How do you meet that challenge?
   - Your curriculum material suggests activities that involve families. Your class is made up of broken homes, blended families, and children who are victims of sad divorces. How would you adapt this for your class?
   - A lesson asks for demonstrations that use expensive items, for instance, fruits and vegetables such as red raspberries, mangos, avocados, and kiwi fruit to demonstrate the colors of the rainbow. You teach in a poverty-stricken area and you yourself are on a very limited budget. How would you adapt?
2. **The teacher.** Teachers differ, too. For example, one likes to involve students in activities, and another is able to get good responses through a teacher-centered lesson. How can the first teacher handle a teacher-centered activity without losing control of the group? What about the second teacher when the material calls for group activities?
3. **The administration.** Pastors, other congregational leaders, and parents will vary in their expectations. What would you do, for example, if they expect extensive memorization of a catechism, but the curriculum materials do not provide for this amount of memory work? Give three suggestions for how to work with this difficulty.
4. **The setting.** Some congregations provide separate rooms that allow for lots of activities, while other classes meet in a small church basement separated by dividers. How could the latter groups handle hands-on activities using tables? Think of three solutions.

Share an incident in your teaching when you made an adaptation. Tell why you made the adaptation and relate how the needs of the students were met and the goal of the lesson was achieved.

Finally, share other ideas for adapting materials. Following are two ideas:

- *Set up enrichment or curricular materials for the quick, eager learners or those who arrive early.* For example, if you are studying about the people of Israel, you could include picture books of Egypt. Or develop individual task cards from which children can choose. One task card could read "Pretend you are Moses. Write a letter to Pharaoh. In the letter, try to persuade Pharaoh to let the children of Israel go." Or print letters (for an acrostic) on the board, such as "God helped me." Students give a word for each letter.
- *Provide resources that help students dig deeply into a lesson.* Bible dictionaries, commentaries, atlases, concordances, and other reference books could be on hand so that students have hands-on time to browse through the books. Give specific assignments or allow volunteers to report some things they learned through their research.

8 Students with Special Learning Needs

GOAL: To learn to recognize learning disabilities and to incorporate those with special needs into the learning environment.

Introduction & Background

Prepare name tags with the words dyslexia, ADD, ADHD, communication challenge, vision challenge, hearing challenge, physical challenge, *and others as submitted by the group. Have participants wear the name tags throughout this session and relate to one another as though the labels are for real. How does their label make them feel? Ask them to listen for various characteristics and needs and to note which ones apply to them with their special learning challenge. At the end of the session have them share with the group their feelings and concerns.*

Just because a person can't speak doesn't mean he or she has nothing to say. Discuss what this means to us as we work with the learning challenged.

A wide range of people experience learning challenges. Not knowing how to respond to the learning challenged may cause discomfort for many. Special communication needs exist for some learners. They have difficulty understanding and using oral language. They may exhibit poor speech, limited vocabulary, "baby talk," or a short attention span. A child with dyslexia may have imperfect directional sense—confusing left and right, up and down. For them *was* is *saw; ten* is *net; form* is *from; left* is *felt; tired* may be *tried; pig* may be *dig;* and so on. Numbers may be similarly reversed.

Sensory challenges include vision or hearing losses. A student with severe vision problems may learn best through tactile and auditory senses; those with a minor loss of vision can use magnifying devices. Encourage lipreading or signing for those with severe hearing challenges. Physical challenges may include significant disabilities in posture and movement due to an accident or disease. These individuals may require assistance from paraprofessionals or peers to fully participate in classroom activities.

Some research shows that as much as 20% of the school-age population may be affected by Attention Deficit Disorder (ADD) or Attention Deficit/Hyperactivity Disorder (ADHD). Some characteristics are inattention, hyperactivity, and/or impulsivity.

Students with learning challenges may change over a period of time with careful instruction. We know of many learning-challenged students of the past who became "greats" in their future. Einstein, a dyslexic child, is a prime example.

Children with learning challenges need prayers, special love, and care. Most of all, they need to know Jesus.

As teachers we will want to help those with learning challenges become accepted members of society, well-loved members in the church who believe and carry the messages of justification and sanctification.

Ideally, we will consider teaching children with challenges to be a special privilege. They have a need to know God. Each of them has some special talent. For example, they may enjoy singing, and they may even be willing to lead a song for the class.

Students with Special Learning Needs

God Speaks

Read Matthew 18:4–6. What childlike quality is Jesus emphasizing? Why is this important for Jesus' kingdom? What challenge does this present to us in our work with learning challenges?

We Respond

1. Does your setting provide appropriate facilities for those with physical handicaps? If not, what accommodations can be made? What accommodations do you make for those with other learning challenges?

2. Many teachers use proximity control—deliberate and calm methods of relating to a child—for students who have been wrongly classified as being impossible to control. What methods have you tried? How well did they work? What could you have done to make them more effective?

3. Collaborate with a student's parents and with school professionals to help understand how an IEP (individualized education plan) has been developed for him or her. Employ as many of the following techniques as possible:
   - Use well-organized and structured activities. Children learn by doing.
   - Give short assignments.
   - Schedule one thing at a time. Be aware of a limited attention span.
   - Remove as many distracting elements from the room as possible.
   - Give positive reinforcement when the student is "attending" during instruction.
   - Use a variety of teaching methods and technology, such as role playing, drama, and videos.
   - Establish realistic behavior expectations.
   - Incorporate motor or movement activities.
   - Collaborate with professionals.
   - Restrict memorizing to important and short materials.
   - concrete materials and objects in contrast to abstract thinking.

4. How have you adapted curriculum materials to meet special needs? Give examples.

5. Did you have problems when you were labeled for this session? Relate your feelings. Also share thoughts you have that would be helpful in working with students who have a learning challenge like the one on your name tag.

6. An important step, as noted above, is to meet with a student's parents or regular classroom teacher (with parental permission) to see what techniques work best with that particular child. These conversations may empower you to teach each learner in a unique way.

 *Adjusting for Individual Differences*

GOAL: To become aware of, identify, and learn how to adjust for individual differences in children we teach.

Introduction & Background

Use an inked pad or washable marking pen to "ink" each person's finger. Stamp the fingerprints on a clean sheet of paper, one fingerprint next to the other. Compare the fingerprints. We are all alike in many ways, but we also have unique differences.

God in His wisdom has created each of us as a unique individual. How fortunate that we are not all clones of one another, each wanting to do the same thing as the other person, each thinking the same things. We each have unique qualities, with interests, talents, and energies running in different paths, so that when all is unified we have a more or less "balanced" society.

Individual differences are explained in many different ways. Some explanations begin with patterns of intelligence. Howard Gardner uses his theory of multiple intelligences, which is divided into *linguistic, logical-mathematics, spatial, bodily-kinesthetic,* and *musical* categories. Others divide intelligence into verbal and nonverbal. What are other kinds of divisions? With these differences come many ways of thinking, seeing, and doing.

As we look over our class we see those who are
- content to sit back, watch, and listen;
- content to sit back and daydream;
- scanners, who like to wander around the classroom;
- energizers, who are enthusiastic and active participants;
- antagonists, very likely to alienate themselves by their behavior; and
- insightful, able to reach far beyond the lesson.

Group members should add others.

We learn by using our various senses. Even though we call upon all our senses, some of us learn more easily with one rather than another. This distinction is made particularly between visual and auditory learners. Each category below suggests ways the teacher can capitalize on these styles.
- Visual: Bulletin boards, banners, posters, reading materials, transparencies, maps, etc.
- Auditory: Video tapes, teacher talk, class discussions, CDs, television, debates, interviews. Students interact with verbalized activities, oral reports, brainstorming, etc.
- Kinesthetic: Touching/feeling objects, manipulating materials, construction, copying materials.

Adjusting for Individual Differences

God Speaks

1. God has given unique talents and gifts to each of us and our students. What blessings does this bring to your class? What challenges?
2. How does 1 Corinthians 10:31 apply to the gifts and talents we and our students have received?

We Respond

Individual differences affect both learning and teaching styles. We seek an optimum match between the learning styles of the student and the strategies of the teacher.

1. The following are teaching styles. The two columns denote opposite types of teaching styles:

____ Indirect, facilitating	____ Direct, teacher-centered
____ Laissez-faire, loosely structured	____ Businesslike, formal
____ Impersonal, distant, disinterested	____ Personal, involved
____ Intense, dramatic	____ Subdued, quiet, restrained
____ Experiential, concrete	____ Abstract, verbal

Place a check mark in front of the teaching styles above that you normally use. Place a plus mark in front of the style you would like to develop more effectively. Are you meeting the needs of most of the students in your class? Why or why not? Select a partner and jot down some of your ideas.

2. Recall one incident when your teaching style did not meet the needs of a student. What was the result? What will you do differently next time?
3. An informal (unscientific) inventory can help us determine whether we learn better by visual or auditory modalities. Of course, we do not draw on all of them (seeing, hearing, feeling, tasting, touching), but we may draw more heavily on one than another. The author has a strong visual modality. Thus, when someone gives her directions to go somewhere, she finds it much easier to follow a map than to follow a list of oral directions.

Try the following informal inventory for fun.

  a. Auditory modality. Read orally the following entries and have students write down each one: 48259; 429268; 6529175; 86537516; 932865914; cup; record; tree; paper; window; chair; door. Stop only one second after each entry.
  b. Visual modality. Print each set of numerals or each list of words on a separate card. Show each card for five seconds before going immediately to the next card. 68435; 396579; 6529175; 91745626; 843917235; apple; tape; glass; pen; basket; notebook; hand.

Allow no repeats or questions. Correct the two informal inventories and compare scores. With which modality did you get a better score? Does that match your analysis of which of these two modalities helps you to learn best or most quickly? What does this tell you as a teacher? (We need to use variety in our presentation styles in our classes to more easily meet the individual differences in our class.)

10 Meeting Children Where They Are

GOAL: To grow in the ability to use instructional practices that take advantage of characteristics of children at various ages.

Introduction & Background

Have each person select a "pretend" age range level from 3–5; 6–9; 10–12; 13–14. Each person introduces himself/herself by giving examples of typical behavior for their age range. The following model might be used for ages 13–14: "My name is Linda. I am sometimes characterized as experiencing severe mood swings and growth spurts. What is my age range?" The group responds to each. Revisit this activity at the end of the session.

Ask participants if they have ever spent hours planning that "perfect" lesson only to have it fall flat. That happens to all teachers at times. Our goals and objectives helped us to know where we were headed, but the stormy weather along the way kept us from reaching the goal.

Could we have prevented the storm by taking the characteristics of the learner into consideration? While a wide range of individual differences exist within each age group, we also find general age characteristics. Photocopy and distribute the list that appears on page 46. Since the list is not exhaustive, you and the participants may choose to add several other characteristics to each group.

Encourage teachers to look for characteristics of children in their reading. Each quarter the introductions of most teachers guides for *Our Life in Christ* (CPH) contain some helpful material. Jane Fryar provides a catalog of characteristics related to teaching religious concepts on pages 71–73 of *Changing Hearts, Changing Lives* (CPH, 1996). Becky Peters summarizes characteristics and appropriate practices on pages 103–4, 117–18, 130–32, 142–43, 155–56 of *Building Faith … One Child at a Time* (CPH, 1997).

As teachers examine the characteristics from page 46, ask them to identify two practical activities to use with a specific story at the age level they teach. Also encourage them to implement Participant Page ideas. Discuss possible implementations as you work through the "We Respond" section.

Meeting Children Where They Are

God Says

1. How does 1 Corinthians 13:11 indicate that we should find different characteristics at different age levels?
2. In spite of our prayers and preparation, we occasionally will have a "downer" lesson. Explain how Isaiah 55:11 comforts you.

We Respond

1. Compare your "pretend" responses in the introductory exercise with the "Characteristics of Children" material. What, if any, are the major differences or similarities?

2. Select a partner who teaches the same age level (or approximately the same age level) as your class. What two practical teaching ideas came to you for a particular story for your age group? Write idea phrases below. Then develop them for the group.

   a.

   b.

   c.

   d.

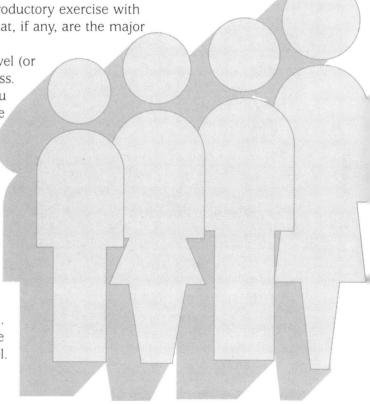

3. Regardless of the characteristics of the age level, affirmation of the students is an important part of teaching. Reflect on the last lesson you taught (or one you will teach soon). Jot down two ways you affirmed or could have affirmed a student for your particular age level.

   a.

   b.

   What reminders can you give yourself so you remember to affirm students in the future? Our students are God's children, just as we are God's children. What does Ephesians 2:10 tell us?

4. Have one person role-play a teacher and one a student in an interactive scene (age level of your choice). *Situation: The student is looking at a comic book and cannot answer the teacher's question because he or she is not paying attention. The student is defiant about being interrupted.* Cut the role play after no more than two minutes. Debrief. How did you (the student) feel when you were "put down" (or other action)? How did you (the teacher) feel when the student treated you with defiance? How would you handle this situation at the various age levels? What would be similarities and what would be differences?

11 How to Use God Language

GOAL: To understand what is meant by "God language" and to learn ways to use "God language" with children.

Introduction & Background

Have participants pretend that they have been asked to tell a non-Christian neighbor, in 25 words or less, what it means to them to be a Christian. They should use appropriate "God language" so she understands them. Then discuss. What concept about God was most difficult to tell to a non-Christian neighbor? What suggestions do participants have for explaining concepts?

When we speak of "God language," we refer to the "lingo" we use when talking about God. We are not talking about a childish or "kiddy" language but a language we use in learning more about God. Can you recall an incident where a child misunderstood the language and had an entirely different interpretation from the one intended? Relate several. For example, a religious journal once displayed a child's cartoon depicting a cross-eyed bear. The child had illustrated the phrase "Gladly the cross I'd bear."

We need to find ways to use the language of our faith so that children will find direction in their lives. Children need opportunities to ask questions and to tell about their belief in their own words instead of just repeating your words without understanding what they mean.

Jesus did not just live long ago and far away. Jesus is here. Jesus is with us today. He will be with us tomorrow. He will be with us forever. We could introduce the word *omnipresent* in this setting. Children hear words in the sermon, and they hear Bible readings, but some of the God language is not part of their vocabulary. However, in the class-room and home we can help them in their journey with God so they learn to better appreciate the mystery of God. Some concepts, of course, we accept by faith.

How do we convey a story to the children so the meaning and understanding are at the child's level? The words we use in the story for the children is a key. We cannot use the same God language for a three-year-old and a middle-school honor student. Their levels of understanding and ability to use abstract terms differ markedly. Thus, we must tailor the God language to the maturity of the class. Review the characteristics of children presented in "Meeting Children Where They Are," pages 24–25 and 46 in this book. These can serve as guides when choosing God language. Also, teachers should check to make sure their class understands the concepts they are presenting.

Checking understanding assumes that we are flexible and open to children's questions, even though we may not have pat answers for all of them. In faith we believe God's message even when we do not understand it. Nevertheless, we strive for understanding. Resources designed to help young children include *Three in One*, by Joanne Marxhausen (CPH, 1973); *Tuck Me In, God,* by Christine Harder Tangvald (CPH, 1998); and *Things I See in Church,* by Julie Stiegemeyer (CPH, 1999).

Finally, encourage teachers to pray and to search the Scriptures. God promises to provide the power we need to present His message with conviction, using appropriate God language.

How to Use God Language

God Speaks

1. Read 1 Peter 3:15. What does this say to us about God language for our children?
2. How would you explain *born again* as used in 1 Peter 1:23?

We Respond

1. What basic things should we know about Christ? According to C. F. W. Walther (as reported by Carolyn Sims in *Winning Friends for Christ* [CPH, 1997], p. 54), we ought to be able to tell
   - How much I need Christ.
   - How much Christ does for me.
   - How I came to faith in Him.
   - Would you add or delete from this list? Why? How would you respond to each of Walther's concepts? In your statements, use language appropriate for the class you teach.
2. In your own words, tell your neighbor what her child would learn about God from you as his or her Sunday school teacher. Use words that are understandable, so both the neighbor and the child can tell you in their own words what you have said. Which words that you use might be difficult?
3. Our body language, too, is important when we talk to others about God. A nonverbal separation from the person occurs if we do not make eye contact with the person while conveying our message. If we tilt back in our chair or continue to read a paper, we give the impression that the message is not important. Tell about a time someone's body language affected the way you heard a message.
4. What do words like *redemption, sanctification, the Trinity, the Sacraments, Law, Gospel, triune God,* and *faith* mean to you? Which of these is the most difficult for you to explain to your class? Ask members of your group to help you do so.
5. Have two persons role-play three different scenes explaining one of the above vocabulary words. One is the conveyor of the message and the other the receiver. Group members should indicate what they see as a lack of communication or nonunderstandable language, if any. The receiver in the role play indicates if anything in the conversation makes him or her feel put down or angry.
6. How will this discussion about God language affect the way you talk about God in your class?

12 Developmental Understandings of Biblical Concepts

Introduction & Background

Ask each participant to identify one childhood quality they would like to recapture. Why? Ask how their responses relate to developing understandings of biblical concepts.

Much of our understanding of biblical concepts rests on our faith. Our journey of faith is lengthy, has many stages and dimensions, and is both simple and complex.

How do we start teaching about faith? It begins in the home, by our example. Families include Bible readings and prayers in their daily devotions. They discuss what has been read, noting how much Jesus loves us and has done for us. Children can bring their own Bible storybook to the devotion and can read from their selection. On special occasions, artwork can follow. In some instances, family members dramatize the story.

Faith continues to grow during bed-time prayers, meal-time prayers, prayers of thanksgiving, and prayers of supplication for ourselves, our family, our neighbors, and the world. We also witness acts of Christian love, such as baking cookies for the refugee family moving in or taking care of the neighbor's one-year-old while the mother undergoes surgery—all for the love of Jesus and our neighbor.

The above speaks of an ideal situation. The reality of broken homes and the unbelievably busy schedules of many family members make it a real challenge to have conversations about biblical concepts, matters of faith, or anything that has not been made a top priority. We cannot trust the culture of today to nourish the faith.

Our students come from a variety of homes. Many do not exemplify a model of Christian faith and love. Our calling in these instances has even greater significance. We want to share the knowledge of God and the way to salvation, to model faith, to touch lives in any way possible, and to develop significant relationships in a Christian community. The home, school, and church can and must work together.

As teachers we look for ways to connect students with the Gospel, through which they grow in their Christian faith. We help them increase their knowledge and understanding of biblical concepts. Faith comes from hearing the Gospel. The Holy Spirit works faith through the Word of God. The faith takes root. The heart, soul, and mind are involved.

Many opportunities exist. They can be as simple as a spontaneous conversation between adults and children who are listening to the birds, smelling the beautiful rose, or seeing the newborn baby—all pointed out as God's special gifts of creation. They will include discussions of sin, forgiveness, and the grace of God in connection with a classroom incident or something that happened in the community last week. They may culminate with activities that apply the Bible story for the day to the lives of the students. By God's grace teachers can use such opportunities to help students grow in their understandings of biblical concepts and—more important—in their faith.

As we seize these opportunities to connect students with biblical concepts, it is important that we consider students' developmental level. See "Meeting Children Where They Are" on pages 24–25 and 46.

Developmental Understandings of Biblical Concepts

God Speaks

Divide into groups and take two Bible passages per group. After returning to the whole group, report what each passage means to your work with children as a teacher of the faith.

1. What does Ephesians 2:8 tell us about our salvation?
2. Knowledge of God is important (Colossians 3:10). However, faith is more than just knowledge of God. How true is the old adage "Faith is not taught; it is caught"?
3. What did Jesus say about welcoming little children in Mark 9:37?
4. How encompassing is the love for God? Read Mark 12:28–30. We do not teach the faith—the biblical concepts—in isolation, with mere "head" knowledge. God's love embraces and encompasses all aspects of life—physical, mental, social, spiritual.
5. Read 1 Corinthians 1:18. How do Christians and unbelievers differ in their interpretation of the message of the cross?
6. What does Deuteronomy 6:6–9 tell us? What meaningful family activities come to mind as you read this?

We Respond

1. Give an example of a challenging biblical concept.
2. Evaluate your pattern of conversation in the home for two days. What opportunities did you have to speak of biblical concepts? Give an example of an opportunity you used. What was the response?
3. Share with the group one incident from one of your classes where a difficult biblical concept took root. If a student made a biblical concept come alive, using his or her own words, relate that also.
4. Write two biblical concepts you will be teaching during the next month or two (or have taught recently). As a group, give helps and ideas to one another for a presentation of the concept to a particular age group.
5. We can help one another conceptualize the meaning of a Bible verse for the day. Have children tell in their own words what the verse means to them. Share an example from your class with the group.
6. Our actions can help to make biblical concepts come alive. How can we touch the lives of children outside the formal education hour on Sundays or weekdays?
7. Identify and apply a biblical concept by having students write a note or letter to someone who is ill, to an elderly person celebrating a special birthday, or to a family member who is dealing with special sadness. Encourage students to write a Bible verse at the bottom or top of the note.

13 Building a Christian Community

GOAL: To build a Christian community in and through Jesus Christ.

Introduction & Background

Give everyone a name tag with someone else's name on it. Form pairs by having participants find the person whose name is on their tag. Stop looking when each person has a partner. (Only one person in each pair will have the partner's name tag.) Have the partners tell what a Christian community has meant to each of them. Then have individuals introduce partners and give a short summary of the interview.

Webster's tenth-edition dictionary defines community as "people with common interests living in a particular area; a group of people with a common characteristic or interest living together within a larger society."

Dietrich Bonhoeffer provides a definition of Christian community in *Life Together: A Discussion of Christian Fellowship* (p. 21): "Christianity means community through Jesus Christ and in Jesus Christ. … We belong to one another only through and in Jesus Christ." Only by God's grace can we live out our Christian commitments in a Christian community. We have been made members of the Christian community and family through Baptism.

Teachers have the opportunity and responsibility to bear and share the Good News with one another in a unique and interdependent faith community. However, many of the children we teach, as well as other team members, may know computers and television better than they know their neighbors or members of the church. We often find children in automobiles rushing from one event to another. Often these events are highly structured and competitive.

The rush of these activities contrasts sharply with time spent in developing meaningful relationships, particularly in a Christian community. Talk with the group about how this picture fits their daily lives. How has it affected their students?

Researchers find that people hunger for meaningful relationships. Some studies have linked "dis-connection" to other human beings to an increase in teenage emotional difficulties and suicides.

These facts highlight the important role of the church in shaping the future of the faith community of our students. We have opportunities to work through our interpersonal relationships and the applications of the traditional teachings in Scripture. We want to relate teachings to contemporary issues of faith and life as much as possible. We do this with mutual forgiveness and deep concern for all in an inclusive rather than exclusive way.

We and our students need to give and receive support from a deep and lasting Christian community in our families, classrooms, and churches. How can we make this happen? The activities we carry out in class cannot succeed on their own. They can, however, make significant contributions. As you discuss this topic, look for practical ideas that involve families and others in the congregation—ideas you can implement immediately.

Building a Christian Community

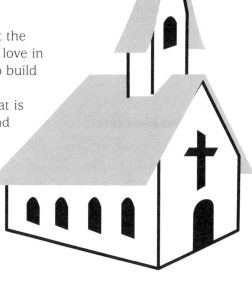

God Speaks

1. What does 1 John 5:1–5 mean to you? What does it say about the way we love the Christian community in our classrooms? Our love in turn reflects on our work with our students in helping them to build community.
2. Acts 2:42–47 gives a model of the fellowship of believers. What is the closest you have come to a support relationship of this kind in your community (your classroom)? Why do you think our church today does not have the same kind of relationships as those of the early Christians?
3. Many influences try to rip down our faith. Christian friends can help us see the love God has shown to us, thereby encouraging us (Hebrews 10:24–25). What opportunities for such encouragement do you have in your class?

We Respond

1. How has your class demonstrated its commitment to building Christian community? What things has it done very well? What areas could be given more attention? What could you as an individual do? What could your students do?
2. What gifts do you bring to the Christian community? What gifts do your students bring? How are these gifts being used?
3. Ask members of your class to reflect on how they got to know one another. Which people in the room know each other best? Why? Who knows each one of them best of all?
4. What keeps you and your students from taking time to cultivate relationships to build community? Discuss with a partner and report your summary to the group. Plan ways to build community.
5. Cliques often form in a class or among religious team members. What could you or others do to show the need to care for people outside of the clique in order to build a stronger community of individuals?
6. Look at the Order of Baptism in your hymnal. What is the relationship and responsibility of the Christian community to each newly baptized member?
7. Prayer is an important part of the Christian community. With another person, write a recipe prayer for community-building in your class. List the "ingredients" that you would put into your recipe for a well-functioning group. At the bottom of your recipe, list three students who you feel would bring the right ingredients to the recipe. How can others be helped to be one of the necessary "ingredients"?
8. Print the following acrostic on the board or on a chart. Record below all of the words submitted by the group that suggest the kind of community you want to have and the kind that God wants you to have. The first letter has been done. Participants are encouraged to reflect on the words during the coming week. Which words call forth an implementation idea for you?

C *aring*
O
M
M
U
N
I
T
Y

14 *Discipline*

GOAL: To gain insight into various kinds of discipline to be used with love.

Introduction & Background

Have a quiet time to see how long everyone can be quiet. Was it hard? Why or why not? Why is it even more difficult for children to be quiet? How quiet should a classroom be for learning to occur?

Some members of your congregation may think the ideal classroom should be breathlessly quiet. Yet we know that some of the best learning takes place in a classroom with the "noise of industry." Quiet classrooms often bore children accustomed to television, computer games, video games, and the like. Teachers, then, face the challenge of controlling the activities that accompany a desirable learning situation.

What are ways to foster a learning atmosphere? The teacher holds the key to much of this. Studies have shown the following characteristics to be important: *enthusiasm, love for children, patience, sense of humor, team player, self-confidence, flexibility, prayerful, well-prepared, good organizational skills, uses a variety of learning-involvement activities, maintains discipline.* Invite participants to add to or delete from this list.

Most teachers find the last one, *maintains discipline,* to be the most challenging. The simple practice of moving around the room can be very helpful. Any practice will be more

effective when it includes *love for children,* a natural outgrowth of the love God has shown to us. Showing love does not mean that we allow children to do almost anything they please. We sometimes use the term *tough love* to describe appropriate teacher behavior. We set boundaries and provide natural consequences when class members go beyond those boundaries. Children feel better about themselves if they have been helped to stay within limits. The other children will not go home after the lesson and say, "It was so noisy in class today that I could not think."

Have participants talk about tough love. How can we achieve a balance between being a drill sergeant and being "nice"? What practices work? What have some tried without success? What suggestions can others give that might enable that practice to be successful?

As you discuss, be aware that no single practice will solve the discipline problems for everyone. Each teacher faces a unique situation that includes the age of children, their family backgrounds, their personalities, the characteristics of the teacher, the lesson plan being used, and the physical surroundings. The good news is that God has promised to be with us and help us at all times. We can count on Him to help us through even the most difficult classroom situation!

Discipline

God Speaks

1. Jesus has special words for our work with children. Describe what He says in Matthew 18:1–5 and 19:13–15.
2. How can Luke 18:13b help you when you feel you have failed to provide the instruction your class needs?

We Respond

1. Evaluate your teaching. Are your expectations of children in your class reasonable under the circumstances? Is your planning adequate? How can it change? Do your lessons lead to fulfillment of goals and objectives?
2. Think of a behavioral challenge in your class.
   a. Did the child understand that what she did or said kept her from full participation and learning more about God? We listen to God's Word so that the Holy Spirit can work in our hearts.
   b. How did the child assess what she did? If it is a deliberate sin, then the teacher applies the Law in love. Praying for forgiveness and asking for help in the future is a quick follow-up.
3. Examine and discuss the classroom procedures on page 47 of this book. These procedures should help to keep children out of simple mischief. We know, however, that there are degrees of mischief—some due to lack of preparedness on the part of the teacher, some due to poor behavior habits on the part of children, some due to the chemistry of the child, some due to misjudgment on our part, and some due to other reasons. In severe cases, you may need parental or colleague involvement to determine how best to work with a particular child. What plan do you have for dealing with serious misbehavior problems?
4. Visit another teacher's classroom, one in which you see real learning taking place. Identify the kinds of behavior the teacher exhibited when all was going according to plan. What did he or she do when there was a disturbance? Was there active involvement by the children? In what types of activities did the children seem most interested, and when did they seem to be learning best? If this were your classroom, what would you do the same and what would you do differently?
5. Avoid "hot spots," or trouble spots. Recognizing your trouble spots is one of the first ways to deal with them. Here are some trouble spots. What are some others that you will want to avoid?
   - Cutting students down
   - Talking back to students
   - Telling students it's okay even when they disturb class
   - Carrying tales to other teachers
   - Getting revenge on disrespectful students

15 Cooperative Learning

GOAL: To gain understanding of the role and application of cooperative learning.

Introduction & Background

Divide into two groups to reflect on the past, present, and future. One group writes a 50-word letter to themselves from their great-great-grandmothers, in which they, the great-great-grandmothers (who lived in the mid-1800s), tell ways in which they gained new knowledge. The other group writes a 50-word letter to their great-great-grandchildren in which they (living at the end of the 20th century) tell all the ways they gain new knowledge. How are the letters the same? How are they different? What role does cooperative learning play in each scenario? (For fun, if you like, ask what the great-great-grandchildren, living at the end of the 21st century, will say about how they gain new knowledge.) Which of the groups (if there are any differences) will rely the most heavily on cooperative learning (in contrast to independent learning)?

This examination of cooperative learning looks at groups. By its very name we can identify at least one characteristic of this kind of learning—cooperation. This contrasts with competition, where students work against one another, trying to be the winner. The implication? The other students are not as good.

In a sense, *cooperative* relates to our faith and Christian life. We support one another. We are not alone; we are a Christian community of faith. The Bible uses terms such as *a royal priesthood, a holy nation,* and *members of the body of Christ.* Our Christian life calls for caring, sharing, trusting, and forgiving one another. Cooperative learning is not a new idea. Jesus and His disciples worked together to achieve a common purpose, such as when He sent His disciples out two by two (Luke 10).

Cooperative learning includes both individual and group goals and accountability. The face-to-face interaction and division of work help students to learn together as brothers and sisters in Christ.

Cooperative learning is yet another way to foster learning. It does not replace other tried-and-true methods of teaching, but does offer unique opportunities for growth.

In summary, cooperative learning fosters cooperation instead of competition. Members of the group work together to accomplish shared goals, interact with one another to clarify difficult concepts and exchange ideas, encourage one another to work hard, grow in their sense of being connected with peers (in contrast to feeling isolation, alienation, or detachment), and build skills of cooperation needed throughout life for service in God's kingdom. Some students feel the security of participating in a small-group setting, in contrast to feeling fear at being "wrong" in a large-group setting.

Certain skills need to be taught in preparation for cooperative learning. Teachers may want to build up to cooperative learning gradually, step by step, week by week. It may be a challenge to have groups understand the importance of cooperative behavior patterns. However, the rewards can be great. How many times have we been in a Bible class, for example, and tuned out while others were in active participation? Cooperative learning requires full participation and repetition. In many cases this leads to heightened interest, superior mastery, and a clearer understanding of the material.

Cooperative Learning

God Speaks

1. As the church, we are a body of believers. See 1 Corinthians 12:7 ("for the common good") and 1 Peter 4:10 ("use gifts received for the common good"). What does this imply about cooperating with others?
2. We do not belong merely to ourselves, and we do not live in isolation. We are incorporated into a family of faith. See Romans 12:3–5.

We Respond

The following sequence can help you gradually begin cooperative learning. For planning, you may want to meet in small groups with other teachers who have classes with students the same age as those in your class. Have discussions, and decide how you will adapt your ideas for your class. Include discussions about room arrangement and the use of materials.

1. *Week one: Learn how to divide into groups.* Decide on the size of groups. Then divide the class into groups by handing out colored slips of paper, drawing a number or letter out of a hat, counting off by number, or dividing by interests. Teach students to move quietly into an assigned place for their groups. Talk about the learning climate that is necessary for group learning. Have students practice speaking in their "soft voice."
2. *Week one or two: Set up the procedures for giving directions and assessing accountability.* Give clear directives to the group by writing on the board, by placing on an assignment sheet, and so on. Spell out goals, objectives, and Bible references in written form so students can refer back to them. Use a few trials the first week. For example, find Bible references. Structure for individual accountability, specify desired behaviors, and explain criteria for success.
3. *Week two or three: Assign jobs or have group members decide on the assignment of jobs within the group.* A leader keeps the group on task. Members have specific assignments, as determined by the group. An encourager can keep the group on task with statements such as "We're really making progress." If a story is used for cooperative learning, each member of the group will receive a special assignment (for example, determine what you think is the main message of the story). Or each participant selects one or two words that they feel carry the main message of a Bible account. A recorder writes down the ideas in the small group and later shares this with the whole group.
4. As the reports are given, the whole-group leader may want to use the chalkboard or poster paper to write down the ideas of each group. Or the group may already have done this and the charts can then be hung around the room. At that time the teacher can be both discerning and encouraging, clarifying if errors have occurred and making adaptations as needed.
5. With a partner address the following questions:
   a. Why would you want to use or adapt cooperative learning in your class?
   b. When might you use cooperative learning?
   c. What benefits will you expect?
   d. What potential problems might you have? What can you do to prevent these problems?
   e. Develop your preliminary plans for introducing cooperative learning below.
   Date:
   Activity:
   Goal(s) to Be Achieved:

   Prevention of Problems:

6. Evaluation. You may not have a perfect lesson the first time. What worked or did not work and why? What adaptations should be made for your group? Be patient.

Participant Page **15**

16 *Portfolios*

GOAL: To gain understanding of the role of portfolios and to gain skill in making portfolios relevant to student learning and growth in Christian faith.

Introduction & Background

Have participants prepare self-portraits in a nontraditional way. Ask, **Who are you? How do you use your talents as a homemaker, a teacher, a dental assistant, a chef, an administrative assistant, an administrator, a computer operator, and so on? Draw yourself on paper in a nontraditional way, by using abstract symbols, creating a recipe, or through some other creative way.**

How can you represent yourself in one of these self-portraits as a child of God? When you are finished, see if others can interpret your self-portrait. Compare this with your own explanation and with other self-portraits of group members as you share with one another. *Then read Ephesians 2:10 and have participants relate to their self-portraits and their role as a Sunday school teacher. God has created us in His image (Genesis 1:27). What does "created in His image" mean to us?*

In the parable of the talents (Matthew 25:14–30), we read of God's workmanship, His expectations of us, and the importance of investing our talents wisely. If Jesus returned today, how much of our potential would He say we are using?

Sunday schoolers are at an early stage in their lives. We expect to help them use their time and talents wisely to grow in their faith as children of God.

Artists have used portfolios for many years to demonstrate their work. Many teachers use them today. They serve as another evaluation tool.

Portfolios are cumulative collections of child and teacher materials. They help give direction to children's lives over time as teachers, students, and parents together prayerfully encourage the child's growth. The portfolio can be a self-portrait of a child at any given time. We can title it "Child of God Portfolio."

Teachers may keep the portfolio materials in an expandable file folder or file box—for a year or longer, perhaps from Nursery Roll to Confirmation, depending on local circumstances. Portfolios may be kept in the church in a storage unit. Keep contents confidential, to be seen only by the teacher, the student, and the student's parents. Students, however, may be given approval to share their portfolio with friends, should they wish to do so.

Place samples of the student's best work into the portfolio. From time to time add teacher comments, photos of the child, recordings of the child reading Scripture or his/her thoughts about a certain aspect of a lesson, and other samples at the teacher's and child's discretion. Keep the portfolio neat and well-organized.

Review the materials at the end of each year and remove some of the samples. Explain the use and purpose of portfolios to parents—individually, if possible—before you begin using them.

Repeat the explanation during the Sunday school period. Involve the parents, letting them know that they may have access to the portfolio with you and their child at any time, or at set times such as in January and again at the end of the Sunday school year. The portfolio can serve as an incentive to follow through with parent conferences. A portfolio can help the child self-assess his or her own progress in the use of time, talents, and growth as a child of God.

Portfolios

God Speaks

Recall the parable of the talents (Matthew 25:14–30). What are some of your talents? How can you use them to the glory of God?

How can you help those you teach to discover the talents God has given them? How might portfolios help?

We Respond

As we work with the portfolio, we want to keep Ephesians 2:8–10 paramount in our minds. Portfolios do not become a tool for boasting, but rather help us recognize with thanks the gifts God has given us. At the same time, they serve as a motivation to carry out God's will to grow as His children.

1. How could the development of a portfolio as a map that leads through a number of months and years of Sunday school be motivational if it is done in a caring, thoughtful way?
2. The following are ideas for portfolio inclusion and teacher discussion. (Suggested age and grade levels are arbitrary. Adapt for your situation.)
   a. Base one of the early entries in the portfolio on a discussion as to what it means to be a child of God. One could use an analogy between our lives and a jigsaw puzzle. Each teacher and child is a piece in the puzzle. What piece would you be? Would your piece "fit in"? Why or why not? With whom does your piece connect? Are you a corner piece (one that helps to get things started) or a center piece? Draw a picture of the jigsaw puzzle.

      Include 10 to 12 pieces. Each piece should have a special connection with you as a child of God. One piece could represent Sunday school, another prayer, and so on. What color should the pieces be and why? (One could use a second jigsaw idea, with each piece labeled with a specific talent. What gifts do I have from God? What things can I already do—walk, talk, sing, think, solve, question, imagine, answer, share, give, etc.?)
   b. Occasionally have the children write a personal quotation from Scripture of their favorite Bible verse for a specific time period. This could well be one of the memory verses and can be written on a cumulative sheet with additions being made throughout the months and years. Provide a small space under each Bible verse where students write why this is a favorite verse.
   c. Include the special activities completed by the child in Sunday school. If feasible, photocopy the activity to send home. Place the original into the portfolio.
   d. Include a potpourri of items, for instance, documentation of the child's role in the annual Christmas service, a copy of a favorite song at a particular age, a description of a participatory role in a skit, and questions the student wanted answered at specific times.

      At various age levels such as grades 3, 5, and 8, students can indicate what they plan to do in life. Is full-time service as a professional worker in the church a consideration? How can God use their gifts? Could some be Sunday school teachers? What concerns did they bring to God in prayer? What do they pray about—difficulties in the family, tensions with friends, someone who is in a wheelchair, and so forth? What are things for which they are thankful? Why? Who is their favorite disciple (record in grades 2, 4, and 6). Why? How have they grown in faith?
   e. Videotape portions of a specific Sunday morning class in grades 1, 3, and 7. Use a small amount of footage each year, but make it cumulative.
3. What immediate action steps can you take to implement the use of portfolios? What needs to happen later?

17 *Understanding Law and Gospel*

GOAL: To grow in understanding of the Law and the Gospel.

Introduction & Background

Talk about laws that affect us in our daily lives. Which laws do we appreciate most? When do we feel condemned by a law? (When we get a speeding ticket?) Has anyone experienced grace in connection with these laws? (No speeding ticket?) Compare these experiences with God's actions in connection with the Law and the Gospel.

We sometimes wish people would not talk about God's Law—or at least that they would not identify specific transgressions of the Law. In a 1998 sermon, a pastor identified abortion and divorce as transgressions of the Law. After church he was immediately confronted and reprimanded, "Don't you know that you are stepping on toes when you mention those transgressions? Some here today may have had abortions or are divorced."

The Law grows not out of God's anger, but out of His love. Without the Law we may think it is possible to save ourselves. But we cannot save ourselves. The Law shows this to be true. God then follows with the Gospel, the good news that faith in Jesus saves us—faith that also is a gift of God's great love. The pastor's sermon included—emphasized—the Gospel. No sinful action is so grievous that it prevents us from being saved! Rather, we repent, receive God's forgiveness, and with His power live according to His will.

Scripture reminds us again and again that we cannot keep the Law perfectly. We all stand guilty. "All have sinned and fall short of the glory of God," Paul writes in Romans 3:23. He continues with the Gospel, "... and are justified freely by His grace through the redemption that came by Christ" (3:24). The Law points us

in the right direction—to the Gospel. We are justified by grace. We also are sanctified—given the power to do God's will—by grace!

In *Changing Hearts, Changing Lives* (CPH, 1996, p. 33), Jane Fryar distinguishes between justification and sanctification as follows:

Justification: God's act of grace in declaring us not guilty—righteous—before Him because of Christ's death on the cross for our sins.

Sanctification: God's act of grace in working in us those thoughts, attitudes, and actions that are pleasing in His sight and that grow out of saving faith.

In *The Christian Faith* (CPH, 1993, p. 107), Robert Kolb states, "The Law describes what life should be like and, therefore, it assesses, analyzes, judges. ... The Law confronts us with our failure to be God's children. In doing so it pronounces judgment. It condemns. It kills. The Gospel, on the other hand, is God's promise that sins are forgiven for Christ's sake, that Christ has fulfilled the absolute demands of God upon humankind, and has restored us to the status of His children through faith. The Gospel saves. It gives life."

In brief summary, the Law teaches us what we are to do and not do; the Gospel tells us what God has done and still does for our salvation.

The Gospel must dominate our teaching, lest we lead students to despair rather than the hope God promises through Christ. However, without the Law students may be tempted to rely upon their own works for salvation. The Law points them to their need for a Savior— the Savior God provided when He sent His only Son into the world.

Understanding Law and Gospel

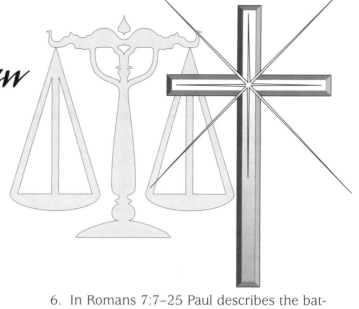

God Says

1. Even though we fail to keep the Law, we rejoice that we are forgiven! What good news do we find in Romans 5:10 and 19?
2. Read 1 Timothy 1:12–17. Why was Paul such an unlikely candidate for preaching the Gospel? How does God's use of Paul encourage you?

We Respond

1. How would you respond to a child who says, "I was so bad today. I can't go to heaven anymore"? What about one who says, "Stop that! You hit me! You hurt me! You are going to hell"?
2. Some have called the Ten Commandments "X rays of the soul." Pretend you have taken an X ray of your soul. How would you diagnose the results? Share, if you like.
3. We read in James 2:10, "Whoever keeps the whole law and yet stumbles at just one point is guilty of breaking all of it." The Law condemns us all! How do you respond to your student who says, "There's no point in even trying to keep the Law, because Scripture says we are guilty anyway, whether we break one law or a hundred"?
4. What is the Law message in Romans 2:14–15? The Gospel message in Romans 10:14–15?
5. Baptism created a "new person." What effect does the "new you" have on your daily life? Tell, if you like, about your old and new natures fighting during the past 12 hours. God works through His Word, Baptism, and the Lord's Supper to make the "new you" grow stronger. What regular opportunities for such growth take place in your life? What are some "new you" activities you can do with your class?

6. In Romans 7:7–25 Paul describes the battle between the "new you" and the "old you" that took place within himself. The Law convicted him of sin, and the Gospel assured him of his salvation. The power of the Gospel also gave Paul the power to live as a follower of God. However, because his "old you" continued to live in him, Paul at times gave in to Satan's power and sinned. The "new you" will recognize the sin, turn to God in repentance, and—yielding to God's power—respond with actions and words of faithfulness to God. Discuss ways to help make children of various ages aware of the daily battle within themselves. Also plan ways to assure them of God's power in that battle and the certainty of the victory that He provides (Romans 7:24–25a).
7. Move into small groups. Each group pretends that you can talk by futuristic communication to someone who will live in the year 3000. (Jot down main points from your conversation on paper so you will remember them when you report to the group.) What would you tell him or her about living and dying almost 1,000 years earlier and being sure about heaven? In the same communication, apply your convictions: faith, Law, Gospel, and "advice" to that person who will be living and dying in the 3000s. Move back into one large group and share your communication. As you listen, look for points you wish you had included in your group's communication.

18 Relevance to the World

This topic includes activities teachers may use with a class of middle-school students.

GOAL: To gain understanding of how a Christian can be in the world but not of the world.

Introduction & Background

Tell participants to hold the Bible in one hand and a mirror in the other hand. Ask how the purposes of these objects are alike and how they are different. (The Bible shows us our spiritual condition; the mirror reflects our outward, physical condition.)

We need to keep in mind what it means to plan for students who are in the world but not of the world. Active learning activities are especially important to help students resist the many temptations in which they find themselves. This topic contains ideas for active learning (in contrast to passive learning). A group of teachers may decide to apply the ideas to their students as well as to themselves.

When we have built relationships with our students, they may tell us that it is a real challenge to "be or see good in a bad world." For example, a movie may give one of your students the feeling that "they will live happily ever after," for evil has been conquered. Yet, when your student comes out of the movie, his bike has been stolen. Biblical passages such as Malachi 4:1–4 reassure us at such times, telling us that in the end God cares for His children.

Some of our students will tell about times when they were in a situation in which they felt they didn't belong. Perhaps their peers were overtly or covertly sinning against one or more of the Ten Commandments. Students may share many of these everyday situations with us and explain why they felt uncomfortable. At times they *will* be tempted by the rationalization, "I knew it was wrong, but everyone else was doing it."

In a sense, we can call Christians "aliens," because we live in the world but are not of the world. It is as though we are in a foreign country; we are in that country, but we are not citizens of the country. *Webster's Collegiate Dictionary,* tenth edition, defines "alien" as "relating, belonging, or owing allegiance to another country or government; differing in nature or character typically to the point of incompatibility." How would our students' lives be different if they were "alien" to Christ and did not know about His forgiveness and salvation?

In Matthew 26:41 we read, "Watch and pray so that you will not fall into temptation." Are we and our students strong enough to resist temptation? Can we think of someone in the Bible who was overconfident? (Such as Peter in Matthew 26:33–35.) We are warned in 1 Corinthians 10:12, "If you think you are standing firm, be careful that you don't fall."

The Holy Spirit works faith in us, and it is through Him that we have the power to lead a Christian life. We are not to "lord over" our non-Christian associates but rather have a relationship of mutual love. At the same time, we must guard against being drawn into the "ways of the world" that are sinful.

In 2 Peter 2:9 and 3:9 we are assured that God "knows how to rescue us" and that He does feel our pain. He sent Jesus for our sins.

Relevance to the World

God Speaks

Read Ephesians 2. God divides our lives into two periods. What are they? Who owned you in the first period and what was the result? Why do Christians still experience the cravings of the past, such as selfishness, lust, and pride? When God made us "alive with Christ" (verse 5), what power did He give us?

We Respond

Select activities below that you can use with your class. Discuss them in advance with other teachers.

1. Have students list ways and forms in which Satan attacked them in their lives during the past week. Point out the power God gives us through the Gospel to resist those temptations. Discuss ways they can receive that power. See, for example, Ephesians 6:11; Romans 6:4; and 1 Peter 5:8–10.

2. Ask which words in the Lord's Prayer ask for protection from the evils of the world. How will these words give encouragement to overcome some temptations during the next week? What are some of the temptations students can expect?

3. Have students make a list of how they want God's help and forgiveness.

Help me, God	Forgive me, God	Thank You, God

4. James 4:4 tells us that "friendship with the world is hatred toward God." James gives guidelines for living the Christian faith on a day-to-day basis. Read 4:7–10 and list four imperatives. Review the source of power we need to follow them and the source of forgiveness when we fail.

5. Have students create a situation in which they have a chance to copy or cheat on their homework, when they lie to their parents about going to a movie, or another situation. Then have students exchange papers and write God-pleasing ways to deal with the situation.

6. Describe this setting to your class: A friend just returned from an overseas trip and enters the room where you are meeting. She says, "Hi. I've been all over the world. I just got back from Ireland. There I viewed war, hatred, and animosity between Christians—Catholics and Protestants." She was appalled and says to the group, "Where have you been this year and what sins against one another as Christians did you see?" Continue until all students have responded one time. Did anyone say, "I did not see hate and animosity. I saw Christians showing their love for one another"? Why or why not?

7. We find idols lurking all around us. Warning signs of idolatry include spending most of our money on material possessions; making excuses for missing wholesome activities, but having time for some that are unwholesome; not considering God and the church to be important. Have students check activities that easily could become an idol for them as individuals:

   ___ television   ___ parties or sleepovers
   ___ shopping
   ___ telephone conversations   ___ clothes
   ___ skateboards   ___ videos
   ___ money   ___ computer games

8. Ask students to write agree (A) or disagree (D) next to the following statements and to briefly explain their answers.

   ___ It is easy to decide if I am conforming to the world and rejecting God.
   ___ Many of my friends serve both Christ and the world.

19 Teacher Satisfaction

GOAL: To find ways to foster teacher satisfaction.

Introduction & Background

Discuss with participants: What jobs do you have in God's kingdom? Which do you enjoy most? Why? How much job satisfaction do you find exists among others on your staff?

We may know individuals we would classify as grumpy. We might say about them, "I don't think they like their job." Fortunately, we also know persons with enthusiasm for their work and a positive attitude. About them we might say, "They have achieved job satisfaction. They are filled with the love of God."

Does a teacher's enthusiasm indicate teacher satisfaction? Some researchers say yes. They find that the teacher's enthusiasm is a better indicator of success than the number of years of experience. Thus, a congregation's educational program can benefit from special attention given to the areas of teacher enthusiasm and satisfaction.

Teachers readily recognize the close relationship between satisfaction and success. They know when their lesson has been a "flat" one. Therefore, teachers who wish to maintain enthusiasm and find satisfaction know what to do: they plan and prepare for each lesson carefully.

Many teachers face obstacles that war against enthusiasm and satisfaction. Time constraints and other commitments prevent them from planning and preparing as they wish they could.

Teachers do most of their planning and preparation on their own, in isolation. Talk with the group about things a group of teachers and others can do *together* to increase enthusiasm and satisfaction. Consider issues such as the following:

What planning and preparation help can teachers receive from others or by working together? What formal and informal meetings might help? What topics could they discuss?

How might the setting for instruction be improved? How can this be accomplished? Who will plan and implement any changes that occur?

What improvements, if any, can be made to the weekly schedule? How would changes affect others? How can the changes be implemented?

What help do teachers receive when they face difficult situations with students or parents? What kind of help do they want? What steps can be taken to provide that help?

How do the personalities of teachers affect one another? Might teachers benefit from an analysis of the personalities of other teachers, especially those with whom they work most closely? Many formal procedures, such as the Myers-Briggs Inventory, help us know ourselves better.

When all is said and done, we need to be sure that we have the proper perspective. Our success, if we want to use that term, comes from God. Perhaps the term *faithfulness* is a better word than success. Paul writes in 1 Corinthians 3:6, "I planted the seed, Apollos watered it, but God made it grow."

Encourage teachers to look for "water" to help them grow. In addition to Bible study and prayer, consider the Internet, study groups, mentoring, and personal inquiry. Many use every opportunity for "shop talk" with colleagues and to visit other classrooms. Professional growth is a key ingredient towards fostering teacher enthusiasm and satisfaction.

Teacher Satisfaction

God Speaks

1. In Luke 13:6–8, Jesus told a parable about the fig tree not bearing fruit. We find a plea: "Leave it alone for one more year, and I'll dig around it and fertilize it. If it bears fruit next year, fine! If not, then cut it down." If you had one more year to change things in your life to make your work more fruitful, what would you do? What "fruit" do you want by next year that you do not have this year?

2. In Matthew 13:3–23 we read the parable of the sower. Relate the four types of soil to "hearers" you have or may have in your class. You may want to think of an analogy to make this come alive for those who do not have background experience with soil.
   - What kinds of worries can choke our growth and take away from teacher satisfaction?
   - What helps to give us deep and flourishing roots so that we are not "deadened" to the needs of those with whom we work?

3. We know that ultimately the growth of the Kingdom depends on the work of the Holy Spirit. How does this relate to teacher satisfaction? If the teacher cannot cause growth, what is our role?

4. Read Galatians 5. Draw out three concepts that are important for growth in teacher satisfaction.

We Respond

1. Write a mission statement that, by God's grace, leads to teacher satisfaction. It could begin, "I believe God is calling me to be ..."

2. You are living in God's Blessed State. Make a license plate on which you identify two special talents you are willing to share in your service in His kingdom. (Many states advertise a special characteristic of their state on their auto license plates.)

3. "Although we plant the seeds in our garden, field, or yard, some take a long while to germinate. Some go into a dormant stage. We cannot make the seeds sprout or grow, although we can nourish them." Consider your work with children and relate one incident that validates this statement. How can this aspect of your teaching add to or take away from your satisfaction?

4. We receive satisfaction from blessings God gives to our work. In addition to the growth we observe during our class sessions, we rejoice when students bring a friend to Sunday school. What can you do to encourage that practice? Consider ideas like thanking students who do so and having an empty chair in the room as a reminder that we have space for a friend.

5. *It takes a lot of preparation to teach just a little.* How does this truth affect your attitude as you prepare to teach a lesson?

6. *Good tools do not make an excellent teacher, but an excellent teacher makes good use of tools.* What additional professional growth opportunities do you wish you had?

20 Your Role as a Member of a Religious-Education Team

GOAL: To gain understanding of and appreciation for the religious-education team.

Introduction & Background

Have participants discuss team experiences from their past. Have any ever felt let down because they did not make a team for which sides were chosen? Our self-worth deteriorates and we feel a lack of acceptance by others. How does it feel to be chosen for a team during the second or third round?

Talents are natural abilities that can be developed and are given by God to all people. These include public-speaking, musical, artistic, and leadership abilities. As Christians we can use these talents to help further the work of the church. Spiritual gifts are special gifts given only to Christians. Paul identifies some of the spiritual gifts in Romans 12:6–8. These gifts flow out of God's work in redemption and sanctification. Like talents, they need to be developed. For some, a talent can become a spiritual gift.

In 1 Corinthians 12:4–6 Paul points out that we use *all* spiritual gifts to serve the Lord. He says, "There are different kinds of gifts, but the same Spirit. There are different kinds of service, but the same Lord. There are different kinds of working, but the same God works all of them in all men." God desires an attitude in which we do not think our gifts are worth more than the gifts of others. Such an attitude will help us work together effectively as a team.

How can it be said that the greatest losses to the church are the buried talents of people? God's chosen people were valuable resources in the church in the past, are so today, and will be in the future. We learn in 1 Peter 2:9 that we are "a chosen people, a royal priesthood, a holy nation, a people belonging to God." Why has God blessed us in this way? The verse continues, "… that you may declare the praises of Him who called you out of darkness into His wonderful light." By God's grace and with His power, we *will* use the gifts and abilities He has given us to serve on His "team."

Thus, all members of the church are people of God. A dynamic parish life involves each of us as members of that parish. As religious-education team members, we are volunteers caring for other people. It is a lifestyle for us in Christ, a response to His mercy rather than a duty. As a member of the team, we take the words of 1 Thessalonians 5:10–11 seriously. Consider reading them together as a group.

When becoming a member of a religious-education team, we take on new responsibilities. We form a new circle of associates and friends. A dedicated member of the team will support the vision of your team leader and the work of other team members. Pray that God will enable that to happen on your team!

Your Role as a Member of a Religious-Education Team

God Speaks

1. God gives spiritual gifts to all Christians. We do not receive them to glorify ourselves, but to build and serve in the church. How does 1 Corinthians 14:12 validate this?
2. Ephesians 1:15, 1:17, 4:1–16, 6:10, and 6:15 list some characteristics for God's team members. Compare these characteristics with those identified at the beginning of the session. How are they the same? Different? Why do you think some people call the Book of Ephesians the "winning team" book?
3. What do 1 Thessalonians 2:4–6 and 5:11 say about our work in God's kingdom and our relationship to one another?

We Respond

1. Divide into groups for five minutes and discuss what qualities you would look for in members of God's religious-education team. Return to the group and make a composite list on the chalkboard or on a chart. How do you know you are a member of God's team, even though you do not have all the qualities on the list? How does your role on God's team differ from your role on a sports team?
2. What does God say about the "in" people and the "out" people in Ephesians 2:1–5? How do these verses help us to understand why we are on God's team even though we do not meet all the criteria identified earlier? How does grumbling about a "deficiency" differ from praying for that same need?
3. When you considered working as a member of the religious-education team, would it have been easy to say, "I'm so overwhelmed. How can I have time?" The devil loves to play that game. He tries to create insurmountable obstacles to our time. We know that time is an irreplaceable gift from God. What are three time "robbers"?

4. On a separate sheet, prepare a list of things you want to start doing, things you want to stop doing, and things you want to continue doing. Share, as you choose, with the group.
5. Because of sin, at times conflict will occur—for instance, conflict between team members or conflict with a parent. Following the conflict-resolution help that Jesus gives in Matthew 18, we go directly to the person. We seek reconciliation though prayer, negotiation, cooperation, and forgiveness. If you are willing, discuss a time of reconciliation that you have experienced.
6. Some observe that people who tend to exclude tend to be excluded. How does this apply to team ministry?
7. Work with partners. Write a job description for a member of the religious team. Include the title, the basic description of the job, supervision arrangements, the term of office, the time commitment, and the responsibilities. Then list the needed gifts, talents, abilities, and training. Have the different team groups share their job description. Refine as necessary.
8. In what areas would you be able to benefit from the help of another person on the team? Privately talk with another team member to arrange the help you need. Also look for ways you can help others.

Participant Page **20**

Characteristics of Children

Preschoolers

Are imaginative, creative, active. Use pantomime, drama, and learner-active involvement; vary activities but also use some repetition.

Like an established routine. Be clear with simple expectations.

Have a natural sense of rhythm. Use singing, clapping, and music activities.

Like touch, smell, taste, look-at, and listen-to activities. Use many multisensory and gross-motor activities; provide objects to handle.

See sins of others more easily than their own; like to tattle. Be a loving, caring teacher to help them feel secure in God's love.

Primary Grade Children

Have new interest in the printed word. Enrich with religious children's books.

Show increased cognitive development. Intersperse activities with quiet, sitting, listening times; use leads such as "I wonder what …"

Like to pretend. Use pantomime, drama, and other learner-active involvement.

Show a wide range of individual differences. Plan some options such as using a variety of supplementary religious children's books.

Are cooperative; like to please. Use children as helpers.

Like rhythms, rhymes, and music. Use poetry, finger plays, and music activities.

Demonstrate internal monitoring of their own conduct. Provide adult direction to help them see God at work in their lives.

Preteen Youth

Are on the threshold of abstract thinking. Introduce supplementary religious children's books; engage in thinking kinds of activities, but intersperse with active involvement.

Are responsible and dependable; want to please. Use volunteers for help.

Like interactive learning with peers. Use some group activities.

Have gained some skill in handling interpersonal relationships. Create times for interacting with peers and helping one another.

See things as right and wrong. Build on this to help them make good decisions.

By grade six, may no longer view school with joy; some have self-esteem problems and are easily embarrassed. Encourage them; stress that Christian self-esteem recognizes that God loves them.

Middle School/Junior High Youth

Want friends and to belong to a peer group. Plan some group activities.

Mimic peer behaviors, clothes, and hair styles; have growth spurts, changes in body chemistry, and identity crises. Be sensitive to changes and the importance of peer relationships; plan activities that include relationship building.

Live in fear of rejection and ridicule. Treat them like adults.

Are excited and frightened as to who they are and where they are going. Guide them in their understanding of the redemptive work of Jesus and their role as a Christian in the world.

Additional Participant Page for

10 *Participant Page*

Classroom Procedures

Some master teachers use the following guidelines to help them keep an orderly class. Place a star in front of the techniques that you already use. Place a check mark in front of those you want to try. Place a minus in front of those you have tried, but they didn't work for you. Add other procedures that you think will help you with your class.

_____ 1. Have the class members help you establish expectations for the class. You will find that most of the time they will be more "strict" than you are. Review these expectations with the class from time to time. Post them and apply them consistently.

_____ 2. Move around the room. Close proximity to the children gives them a crutch to "stay in line."

_____ 3. Maintain eye contact with the children. While you are physically moving around, keep your eyes moving around also so children know you care about their attention. As much as possible, do not turn your back to the children.

_____ 4. Use consistent approaches. For example, raise your hand with two fingers pointing up or turn out the light for a moment as a signal for quiet time.

_____ 5. Be prepared at all times, have materials laid out in sequential order, know what you are going to do, and have creative ideas ready to go and be sure they are age-appropriate.

_____ 6. Intersperse your presentation with questions; keep the children involved.

_____ 7. Check the seating arrangement. Should it be changed? Reinforce good behavior.

_____ 8. Vary the activities. Use as many active-involvement learning activities as possible.

_____ 9. Use children's names in all of your relationships.

_____ 10. If possible, do not stop the lesson; don't allow it to erode if an infraction takes place. Try using eye contact or quietly calling a name as a reminder of an infraction.

_____ 11. Keep a sense of humor and perspective. Show respect for the children. Do not use sarcasm.

_____ 12. Be firm and confident. Let the children know that you are calmly in charge and consistent in your expectations.

_____ 13. Pray for the Lord's guidance and for each child in your room. The temptation of sin is always there.

_____ 14. _____

_____ 15. _____

Discuss these procedures with other teachers. Which have you found to be most important? What variations have worked for you? What other procedures do you suggest?

Additional Participant Page for

Participant Page **14**